IOI MEN IN
KILTS

Photographs by Bob McDevitt

BACKPAGE

3rd Edition – May 2019
First published in October 2017

BackPage Press
49-53 Virginia Street
Glasgow, G1 1TS
www.backpagepress.co.uk

A CIP catalogue reference for this book is available from
the British Library.

ISBN 9781909430297

Printed and bound by Hussar Books, Poland

BOB

50
Photographer, Glasgow

CONTENTS

Jack	6	Blair	62	Donald	118	Arkadiusz	174
Ollie	8	Stevie	64	Ross	120	Woody	176
Blair	10	Justin	66	Mark	122	Atta	178
Ande	12	Steven	68	Patrick	124	Alessandro	180
Paul	14	Andrew	70	David	126	Neil	182
Steven	16	Stewart	72	Dominic	128	Kevin	184
Andrew	18	Crawford	74	Daniel	130	Greig	186
Robbie	20	Stuart	76	Keith	132	Ian	188
Jonny	22	Greg	78	Derek	134	Martin	190
Ashton	24	Jack	80	Lawrence	136	Fraser	192
Nathan	26	Paul	82	Billy	138	Niall	194
Chris	28	Alex	84	Jacob	140	Thomas	196
Craig	30	Paul	86	Dean	142	Darren	198
Michael	32	Colin	88	Craig	144	Martin	200
Owen	34	Daniel	90	Alex	146	Andrew	202
Gary	36	David	92	Keir	148	Jack	204
Drew	38	Graham	94	Scott	150	Andrew	206
Chris	40	Colin	96	Kevin	152		
David	42	Dominic	98	Grant	154		
Colin	44	Paul	100	Brendan	156		
Paul	46	David	102	Philip	158		
Iain	48	Gavin	104	Stephen	160		
John	50	Joe	106	Elliot	162		
Sean	52	Gylen	108	Ryan	164		
Hunter	54	Paul	110	Antony	166		
Iain	56	Barry	112	Aly	168		
Stuart	58	Akintunde	114	Jonathan	170		
Dave	60	Jonathan	116	Alan	172		

JACK

21

Musician, Glasgow

OLLIE

35

National Park Ranger, Helensburgh

BLAIR

35

Master Barber, Cumbernauld

ANDE

35

Bike Mechanic, Daliburgh, South Uist

PAUL

38

Surgical Sales Manager, Stirling

STEVEN

26

Acrobatic Coach, Glasgow

ANDREW

48

Retail Manager, East Kilbride

ROBBIE

31

Publisher, Wighton

JONNY

26
Model, Glasgow

ASHTON

27

Account Manager, Carrickfergus

NATHAN

29

Youth Worker, Dunblane

CHRIS

37

Choreographer, Glasgow

CRAIG

22

Actor, East Kilbride

MICHAEL

47

Assistant Director (Film/TV), Glasgow

OWEN

28

Student, Bridge of Allan

101 Men in Kilts

GARY

25

Mental Health Nursing Student, Blackwood

101 Men in Kilts

DREW

27

Trainee Solicitor, Glasgow

CHRIS

24
Personal Trainer, Glasgow

101 Men in Kilts

DAVID

27

Charity Trustee, Dumbarton

COLIN

40

Photographer, East Kilbride

PAUL

21

Student, Elderslie

IAIN

36
Police Officer, Paisley

JOHN

58

Company Director, Glasgow

SEAN

18

Student, Galston

101 Men in Kilts

HUNTER

37

Service Manager, Paisley

IAIN

39

Engineer, Glasgow

STUART

24

Purchasing Group Leader, Aberdeen

DAVE

30

Trainee Teacher, Glasgow

BLAIR

25

Actor, Dumfries

STEVIE

58

Publishing Sales Manager, Glasgow

JUSTIN

33
Teacher, Glasgow

STEVEN

34

Estate Agent, Kilmacolm

ANDREW

29

Actor, Ayr

STEWART

32

Violinist, Lundin Links

CRAWFORD

25

Singer/Songwriter, Glasgow

STUART

24

Founder, SolarVis Technology, Kilbirnie

GREG

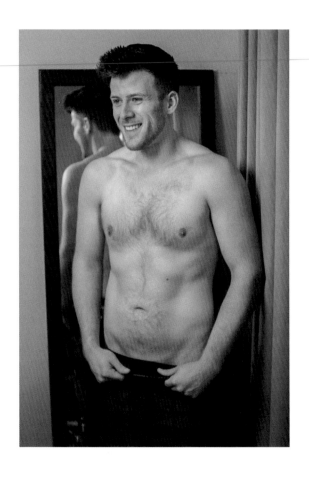

26

Choreographer, Cumbernauld

JACK

21

Actor, Armadale

PAUL

43

Actor & Model, Renfrew

ALEX

30

Logistics Manager, Peterhead

PAUL

27

Photographer, Dunblane

COLIN

32

Actor, Paisley

DANIEL

28

E-Commerce Administrator, Glasgow

DAVID

26

Postman, Elderslie

GRAHAM

51

Filmmaker, Stornoway, Isle of Lewis

COLIN

28

Teacher, Blackwood

DOMINIC

45

Teacher, Newport-on-Tay

PAUL

38
Actor, Glasgow

DAVID

26

Traceur, Tobermory, Isle of Mull

GAVIN

39

Personal Trainer and Massage Therapist, Larkhall

JOE

29

Actor, Glasgow

GYLEN

36

Video Producer, Inverness

PAUL

28
Software Engineer, Glasgow

BARRY

30

Project Analyst, Edinburgh

AKINTUNDE

31
Volunteer, Glasgow

JONATHAN

53

Public Sector Director, Carluke

DONALD

40

Technical Services Manager, Strathaven

ROSS

25

Lifeguard, Dumfries

MARK

45

TV Producer, Glasgow

PATRICK

24
Actor, Glasgow

DAVID

25

Trainee Social Worker, Cumbernauld

DOMINIC

27

Singer, Newcastle

DANIEL

25

Actor, Glasgow

KEITH

31

Fashion Designer, Glasgow

DEREK

48

Fitness Instructor, Glasgow

LAWRENCE

23
Health Professional, Bellside

BILLY

57

NHS Practitioner, Easterhouse

101 Men in Kilts

JACOB

22

Actor, Edinburgh

DEAN

35

Mixed Martial Arts Coach, Clydebank

CRAIG

23

Student, Glasgow

ALEX

37

Music Teacher, Rugby

KEIR

18

Acting Student, Perth

SCOTT

25

Instrument Technician, Rural Stoneywood

KEVIN

33
Doctor, Dalgety Bay

GRANT

42

Workshop Manager, Dunblane

BRENDAN

40

Doctor, Helensburgh

PHILIP

35

Bus Driver, Maryport

STEPHEN

24

Multimedia Designer, Bishopbriggs

ELLIOT

25

Retail Manager, Falkirk

RYAN

18
Musician, Dunblane

ANTONY

34
Sales Team Leader, Stirling

ALY

42

Library Sales Manager, Edinburgh

JONATHAN

22

Professional Cyclist, Paisley

ALAN

56

Writer, Girvan

ARKADIUSZ

35

Economist, Świebodzice

WOODY

31

Finance Manager, Glasgow

ATTA

38

Actor, Glasgow

ALESSANDRO

28

Actor and Director, Glasgow

NEIL

36

AV Technician, Stirling

KEVIN

40

Senior Financial Accountant, Mwanza, Tanzania

GREIG

46

Interiors Manager, Rothesay, Isle of Bute

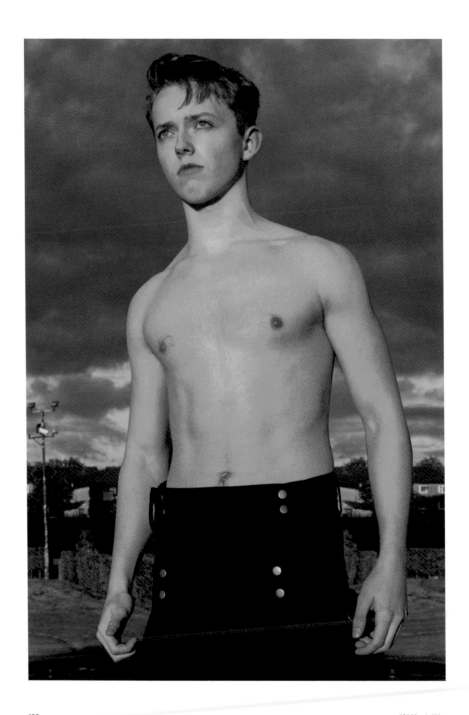

101 Men in Kilts

IAN

19

Student, Johnstone

MARTIN

34
Makeup Artist, Lilliesleaf

FRASER

19

Sound Engineer, Glasgow

NIALL

28

Journalist, Cumbernauld

THOMAS

23
Project Manager, Edinburgh

DARREN

26

Doctor, St. Andrews

MARTIN

38

Publisher, Glasgow

ANDREW

27

Cellist, Breakish, Isle of Skye

JACK

26
Doctor, St. Andrews

ANDREW

25

Trainee Surveyor, Dunblane

ACKNOWLEDGEMENTS

I'd like to thank the following people who helped make this book happen. First of all to my 101 men, who gave their time and energy and really entered into the spirit of the project.

Dave Cooke at Pantheon Theatre (pantheontheatre.co.uk), Keith Malloy at Electro Rebel (shopelectrorebel.com) and June Young at That Looks Good Costume Hire (thatlooksgood.com) who all helped out with kilts.

Martin and Neil at BackPage Press for their publishing skill and expertise and Nick and Davinder at Freight Design (freightdesign.co.uk) for their creativity and patience.